Latin American Celebrations
and Festivals

Day of the Dead
Día de los Muertos

Kerrie Logan Hollihan

**Traducción al español:
Ma. Pilar Sanz**

PowerKiDS press. & **Editorial Buenas Letras**™
New York

Published in 2010 by The Rosen Publishing Group, Inc.
29 East 21st Street, New York, NY 10010

First Edition

Editor: Nicole Pristash
Book Design: Greg Tucker
Photo Researcher: Jessica Gerweck

Photo Credits: Cover R. H. Productions/Getty Images; p. 5 David Hiser/Getty Images; p. 7 © Barbara Heller/age fotostock; p. 9 © Mauricio Ramos/age fotostock; p. 11 Shutterstock.com; pp. 13, 21 Lawrence Migdale/Getty Images; p. 15 Herman Agopian/Getty Images; pp. 17 (main),17 (inset) Omar Torres/AFP/Getty Images; p. 19 Luis Acosta/AFP/Getty Images.

Library of Congress Cataloging-in-Publication Data

Hollihan, Kerrie Logan.
  Day of the Dead = Día de los Muertos / Kerrie Logan Hollihan ; traducción al español, Ma. Pilar Sanz.
— 1st ed.
      p. cm. — (Latin American celebrations and festivals = Celebraciones y festivales de latinoamérica)
Includes index.
  ISBN 978-1-4358-9363-4 (library binding)
  1. All Souls' Day—juvenile literature. I. Title. II. Title: Día de los muertos.
  GT4995.A4H65 2010
  394.266—dc22
                                        2009029083

Manufactured in the United States of America

CPSIA Compliance Information: Batch #WW10PK: For Further Information contact Rosen Publishing, New York, New York at 1-800-237-9932

CONTENTS

CONTENIDO

As October ends, children in Mexico and other Latin American countries start to smile. It is time to celebrate *Día de los Muertos*, or Day of the Dead. On the first two days of November, families gather to remember their loved ones who have died.

Cuando octubre se acerca a su fin, los chicos y chicas en México y otros países de Latinoamérica comienzan a sonreír. Es tiempo de celebrar el Día de los Muertos. En los primeros dos días de noviembre las familias se reunen para recordar a sus seres queridos que han muerto.

People of all ages come together to celebrate during Day of the Dead.
Gente de todas las edades se reúne para celebrar el Día de los Muertos.

Day of the Dead dates back to early groups of people in Mexico, such as the Aztecs. They believed that the spirits of the dead traveled back to Earth once a year. These early groups left offerings of flowers and fruit to help the spirits on their way.

El Día de los Muertos se remonta a los primeros habitantes de México, como los aztecas. Los aztecas creían que el espíritu de los muertos regresaba a la Tierra una vez al año. Los aztecas dejaban flores y frutas para ayudar a los espíritus en su camino.

This is a figure of Mictlantecuhtli. The Aztecs believed that he ruled the land of the dead.

Los aztecas creían que Mictlantecuhtli (arriba) dominaba el mundo de los muertos.

Catholics from Spain came to Mexico in the 1500s. Catholics remembered their dead on November 1 and 2, All Saints' Day and All Souls' Day. Mexicans mixed their celebration with the Catholic celebration. Together, these two celebrations became Day of the Dead.

Grupos de católicos de España llegaron a México en los años 1500. Los católicos recuerdan a sus muertos durante el Día de Todos los Santos, y el Día de los Fieles Difuntos, el 1 y 2 de noviembre. Los mexicanos combinaron su celebración con las fiestas católicas. Estas fiestas se convirtieron en el Día de los Muertos.

Catholics built missions to spread their beliefs. This is Conca Mission in Querétaro, Mexico.

Los católicos construyeron misiones en México para transmitir sus creencias.

During Day of the Dead, families set up an *ofrenda* (oh-FREN-da), an **altar** to remember loved ones, in their homes. Families set photos of the dead there. Children write notes and draw pictures. Sometimes, families place ofrendas on **graves**, as well.

Durante el Día de los Muertos, las familias ponen ofrendas, o **altares**, en sus casas para recordar a sus seres queridos. En los altares se colocan fotografías de los muertos. Los niños escriben notas y hacen dibujos. A veces, las familias ponen las ofrendas en las **tumbas** de sus familiares.

Here you can see an ofrenda that a family has set up on their loved one's grave.

Aquí vemos una ofrenda que una familia ha colocado en la tumba de sus seres queridos.

Ofrendas are loaded with offerings such as **skulls** and small toys. Rows of colorful paper cutouts called *papel picado* (pa-PEL pee-KAH-thoh) fly from strings. Marigolds welcome the spirits. Many believe that the spirits look for these bright yellow flowers!

Las ofrendas tienen muchas sorpresas, tales como **calaveras** y pequeños juguetes. El papel picado cuelga de los techos y adorna las mesas. Las flores de cempasúchil reciben a los espíritus. Muchos creen que esas brillantes flores amarillas atraen a los espíritus.

Sugar skulls, like this one, are common during Day of the Dead. Skulls represent death.

Las calaveras de azúcar son muy comunes durante las fiestas del Día de los Muertos.

During Day of the Dead, families cook foods that their loved ones liked. When visitors come, everyone eats. They feast on **tamales** made with meat, cheese, or nuts. They snack on fruit and sweets. Children write their names on sugar skulls. Some kids take a bite!

Durante el Día de los Muertos se cocina la comida favorita de los seres queridos que han muerto. Los visitantes comen **tamales** con carne, quesos y nueces. Además se comen dulces y frutas. Los niños escriben sus nombres en calaveras de azúcar. ¡Muchos niños se comen sus calaveras!

During Day of the Dead, family members often make their loved one's favorite food together.
En el Día de los Muertos las familias cocinan los platillos favoritos de sus seres queridos.

15

When Day of the Dead arrives, bakers sell *pan de muerto* (PAHN DEH MWER-toh), or bread of the dead. Many bakers put a small, round piece on top that is meant to be a skull and skinny pieces on the sides that are meant to be bones.

Cuando llega el Día de los Muertos los panaderos venden "pan de muerto". Muchos panaderos ponen una pequeña forma redonda sobre el pan que representa una calavera. Otras piezas delgadas sobre el pan representan los huesos.

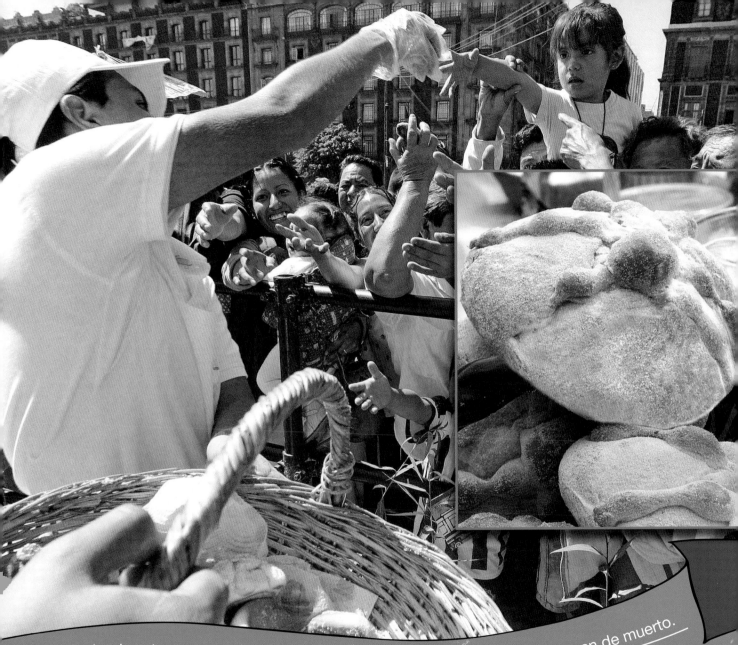

A baker hands out pan de muerto in Mexico. *Inset*: A close-up picture of pan de muerto.
Un panadero vende pan de muerto en México. *Recuadro*: un detalle del pan.

This celebration is a time to make people laugh. People write short poems that make fun of famous men and women. Musicians sing and play. Artists dress **skeletons** in clothes and position them in ways that make them look like they are playing ball, shopping, and driving!

El Día de Muertos es hora de reír. La gente escribe pequeños poemas que hacen burla de personas famosas. Los músicos entonan canciones. ¡Los artistas visten **esqueletos** de forma divertida jugando al fútbol, manejando un automóvil o yendo de compras!

La Catrina, shown here, is a skeleton that is a symbol of Day of the Dead in Mexico.

Aquí vemos a la Catrina, un esqueleto que representa al Día de los Muertos en México.

Day of the Dead is being celebrated more often in the United States. Mexican Americans build ofrendas and eat pan de muerto. Children play with toy skulls and paper skeletons. Mexican Americans and other Latinos spend this holiday with loved ones.

El Día de los Muertos se celebra cada día más en los Estados Unidos. Los mexicoamericanos hacen ofrendas y comen pan de muerto. Los niños juegan con calaveras de juguete y esqueletos de papel. Muchos mexicoamericanos y otros latinos en los Estados Unidos celebran el día de los muertos con sus seres queridos.

Day of the Dead is a happy holiday spent with family.

El Día de los Muertos es un día feliz para pasarlo con la familia.

21

The skulls and skeletons of Day of the Dead might seem scary. However, Latin Americans find great joy in this holiday. They think about people they once knew and still love now. During Day of the Dead, people celebrate life and death as important journeys.

Las calaveras y los esqueletos del Día de los Muertos parecen dar miedo. Pero, los latinoamericanos encuentran gran gozo en esta celebración. Es tiempo de recordar a los seres queridos. Durante el día de los muertos se celebra el importante camino entre la vida y la muerte.

Glossary

altar (OL-ter) A table or a stone on which offerings are made.

graves (GRAYVZ) Places where dead people are buried.

skeletons (SKEH-leh-tunz) What gives animals' or people's bodies shape.

skulls (SKULZ) The bones in animals' or people's heads that keep their brains safe.

tamales (tuh-MAH-leez) Dishes made of corn dough that are stuffed with certain things.

Glosario

altar (el) Una mesa o piedra en la que se colocan ofrendas.

calaveras (las) Los huesos de la cabeza, en las personas y animales, que protegen el cerebro.

esqueleto (el) Los huesos que le dan forma a las personas y animales.

tamales (los) Un platillo realizado con masa de maíz rellenos de carne o verduras.

tumbas (las) Lugares donde se entierra a las personas.

Index

Índice

Web Sites / Páginas de Internet

Due to the changing nature of Internet links, PowerKids Press has developed an online list of Web sites related to the subject of this book. This site is updated regularly. Please use this link to access the list:
www.powerkidslinks.com/lacf/dead/